Listen Here!

Intermediate Listening Activities

Previously published by Georgian Press

Clare West

CAMBRIDGE
UNIVERSITY PRESS

University Printing House, Cambridge CB2 8BS, United Kingdom

Cambridge University Press is part of the University of Cambridge.

It furthers the University's mission by disseminating knowledge in the pursuit of education, learning and research at the highest international levels of excellence.

www.cambridge.org
Information on this title: www.cambridge.org/9780521140348 (without key)
www.cambridge.org/9780521140362 (with key)

First published by Georgian Press (Jersey) Limited 1999
Reprinted and published by Cambridge University Press 2010
3rd printing 2013

Printed in the United Kingdom by Short Run Press, Exeter

A catalogue record for this publication is available from the British Library

ISBN 978-0-521-14034-8 Paperback without key
ISBN 978-0-521-14036-2 Paperback with key

Cambridge University Press has no responsibility for the persistence or accuracy
of URLs for external or third-party internet websites referred to in this publication,
and does not guarantee that any content on such websites is, or will remain,
accurate or appropriate. Information regarding prices, travel timetables and other
factual information given in this work is correct at the time of first printing but
Cambridge University Press does not guarantee the accuracy of such information
thereafter.

Produced by AMR Design Ltd (www.amrdesign.com)
Drawings by David Birdsall, Tony Jones and Rania Varvaki
Cover image: © Shutterstock

CONTENTS

The Tapescripts begin on page 65 of the With Key edition.
The Key begins on page 88 of the With Key edition.

INTRODUCTION

Listen Here! is for students at lower intermediate to intermediate level who want to improve their listening in English. It also offers useful practice to those preparing for the Cambridge Preliminary English Test (PET). It can be used to supplement any coursebook at this level, and is suitable for use in the classroom, or in the case of the With Key edition, for self-study.

Listen Here! provides:

- over 2½ hours of recorded material on two C80 cassettes
- lively recordings in standard and regional British English
- occasional American and Australian voices
- a wide range of topics taken from the PET syllabus
- a variety of tasks for active listening
- additional speaking and pronunciation practice
- a simple, attractive layout, so that the material is easy to use.

How is the book organised?

There are 28 double-page topic-based units. Each unit consists of two recorded texts with a number of activities, a pronunciation or speaking exercise, and sometimes a listening tip. The Tapescripts and the Key are at the end of the With Key edition.

There is an index to the Pronunciation and Speaking exercises, and also a Pronunciation Bank to help students with unusual or difficult words, especially place names.

How should Listen Here! be used?

Teachers using the book as supplementary material should feel free to dip in and out of the units as they wish. However, the units are graded in order of difficulty, starting with the easiest, so students studying on their own should work through the units in order. Later units have more difficult texts, or more difficult tasks. A gradual approach will help to build up skills and confidence.

Tips for the teacher

This book aims to reflect what happens in the classroom and real life, by adopting an integrated approach to the skills of listening and speaking. A purely listening lesson may become stressful and tense, with the whole class listening silently, nervously and unprepared for the correct answer. Instead, communicative activities can be used to introduce the topic orally, which will help to put students in the most receptive mood for listening, and feedback can be lively and enjoyable.

Choose units that you feel are appropriate for your class's listening level and general interests. Use Part A as a warm-up or to predict or present vocabulary or ideas that will be needed in the rest of the unit. Then move on to Part B. Allow students time to look at the rubric first, and

then play the recording as often as necessary. You will have to rewind the tape, as each recording appears only once (except in the Pronunciation exercises in Part D).

Encourage plenty of feedback and discussion in pairs or small groups and the whole class, before moving on to Part C. In most units this involves a new recording and new tasks, still on the same theme. Leave a little time at the end of the lesson for the Speaking or Pronunciation activities (Part D in most units). Many teachers find that a brief but regular focus on stress, intonation and pronunciation is the best way to improve students' ability to make themselves understood, as well as their ability to understand other people.

Tips for the student

- Start with Unit 1, or choose another unit in the first five if you prefer. Look at the title, and think about the topic for a few minutes (in English!).

- Work through the unit, listening to the tape as often as you like. You will have to rewind the tape each time you want to listen to a recording again (except in Part D).

- If you are alone, practise the speaking exercises by speaking aloud to yourself. Practise the pronunciation exercises in front of a mirror, so that you can see exactly how your mouth and lips are moving.

- Don't forget to read and think about the Listening Tips at the end of some units. You may find the Pronunciation Bank at the end of the book useful, too.

- The more often you listen to a recording, the more you will understand, so listen to it on your walkman, in your car or at home, if you can.

Finally ...

I hope you all enjoy using *Listen Here!*

CLARE WEST

This book is dedicated to my daughter Leila.

1 FACTS AND FIGURES

Do you find it easier to remember facts or figures? Look at this box for 30 seconds and memorise as much as you can.

The capital of Australia is Canberra.	23 September 1913
The Globe Theatre was burned down in 1613.	4879133
Red hair is stronger than blond hair.	01772 651504

Close your book and write down what you remember, or tell your partner. If numbers are more difficult for you, can you think of any ways of making them easier to remember?

B1

A teacher wants to arrange accommodation for a group of students on a farm. Listen to his phone conversation and tick (✔) the correct sentences.

1 The teacher has a small group of students.
2 Accommodation at Mill House Barns is cheap.
3 Bathrooms and hot water are available.
4 The students are used to better living conditions.
5 Everything is provided.
6 The students are going to stay there for four nights.
7 It is necessary to pay in advance.
8 The teacher is pleased with the arrangement.

B2

Listen again and complete the teacher's notes.

Mill House Farm   Owner: _____
No. of students _____
Cost per student _____
What about beds? _____
   „   washing facilities? _____
   „   food?   Do own cooking
Students must bring with them _____
No. of nights _____
Dates _____
Time of arrival _____
Total cost _____
How to pay? _____
When? _____

C1

Listen to the conversation about general knowledge and circle the correct answers (A, B or C).

1 Who was the first man on the moon?
  A Yuri Gagarin
  B Buzz Aldrin
  C Neil Armstrong

2 Which country has the most TV sets?
  A USA
  B China
  C Japan

3 What's the most expensive film ever made?
  A *Gone with the Wind*
  B *Jurassic Park*
  C *Titanic*

4 Who sailed across the Pacific on a raft?
  A Francis Chichester
  B Thor Heyerdahl
  C Robert Scott

5 How many hairs are there on the average human head?
  A 1,000,000
  B 1,000   C 100,000

6 Who was the youngest ever Wimbledon tennis champion?
  A Martina Hingis
  B Boris Becker
  C Michael Chang

C2

Listen to these phrases from the recording and choose the correct words or phrases you hear from the pairs in the box.

1 haven't ever / haven't even
2 we only need about / we only need a boat
3 shall we start / should we start
4 who first stepped / who first tapped
5 wouldn't they / mightn't they
6 no, my dear / no idea
7 actually / really
8 on a raft / on or after
9 a member – him / remember him
10 I should say / I should think

D

PRONUNCIATION PRACTICE: Dates and numbers

Listen and repeat these dates and numbers after the speaker.

6 AD   1066   1872   1901   1924   the year 2000
25th May   14th February   December 11th   1st June   3rd March
1,000,000   100,000   1,000   1,001   132   89
13   30   15   50   17   70   18   80   19   90
557216   643801   9473862   525813   296017   *(telephone numbers)*

Listening tip   Listen extra carefully to numbers, dates and names. Always check if you aren't sure, for example: *'Sorry, was that 16 or 60?'* *'Did you say June or July?'* *'Do you spell it with an i or not?'* *'Is it 772138 or 772148?'*

2 HAVING FUN

A Which activity in these pictures would you prefer, and why?

A   B   C

B1 When Ted comes home, he finds three recorded messages on his answerphone. Read the sentences, then listen and choose from A, B or C to complete the sentences correctly.

1 The messages are all A invitations B complaints C instructions.
2 Ted is A a film student B a dancer C a manager.
3 Donald Ferguson is A Ted's friend B Ted's boss C Ted's neighbour.
4 Carol is A Ted's girlfriend B Ted's wife C Ted's sister.
5 The times mentioned are A mostly for this week B only for this week
   C mostly for next week.

B2 Listen again and complete the information in Ted's notebook.

1	From: _____	When: _____	M
	About: seeing a film	What time: _____	E
	Where: the Odeon	Where to meet: _____	S
			S
2	From: Donald Ferguson	When: _____	A
	About: _____	What time: _____	G
	Where: _____	Dress: not formal	E
			S
3	From: Jason	When: _____	
	About: _____	What time: _____	
	Where: his place	Address: _____	

C1   Listen to two people, Sophie and Sally, arranging a party. Read the questions, then listen and choose the correct answer (A, B or C).

1   Who is leaving?   A Thomas   B Trevor   C Terry
2   Who is going to book the restaurant?   A Sally   B Sophie   C Susie
3   Which restaurant is it?   A Othello   B Otello's   C O'Dells
4   How many people will be at the dinner?   A 50   B 15   C 55
5   What time will the booking be for?   A 7.00   B 7.15   C 7.30
6   How long has Trevor worked for the company?   A 14 years   B 10 years   C 4 years
7   What extra thing should the restaurant provide?   A a cake   B a special dish
    C a plate with his name on
8   What are they thinking of doing after the dinner?   A going home   B singing
    C dancing

C2   Listen again and find the exact words which are used instead of the phrases or sentences below.

1   In two weeks' time.
2   I'll do it immediately.
3   I hope they aren't fully booked.
4   How long has he worked here?
5   We'll give him a good farewell party.
6   I like the sound of that!

D   PRONUNCIATION PRACTICE: Word and sentence stress

Listen to these sentences and underline wherever you hear a strong stress. Number 1 is done as an example.

1   I'll <u>see</u> you to<u>mo</u>rrow.
2   She posted the letter last night.
3   The present? Oh, give it to him!
4   The piano was sold for a hundred pounds.
5   When does the bank close?
6   He'll set the table for you.
7   I bought a really beautiful jacket there.
8   Sit down and have a cup of coffee.

Listen again, and repeat after the speaker.

Listening tip

If you have difficulty breaking English up into groups of words you can recognise, listen for stress, which is usually on nouns and verbs. Many of the unstressed sounds are not important for general understanding.

3 SOUNDS DELICIOUS!

Think about or discuss these questions about food.

What kind of food do you like? Is there any food you dislike?
Do you eat meat, or are you a vegetarian?
Do you eat just one big meal a day, or several small meals or snacks?
Do you sometimes go out to eat? What types of restaurant do you like?
Can you cook? What are your specialities?

B1

**You are going to hear somebody giving a friend a recipe for making soup.
Listen and tick (✔) the types of food that you hear.**

apple	carrots	cucumber	milk	potatoes
beef	cheese	lemon	mushroom	salmon
bread	chicken	lettuce	oil	tomatoes
butter	courgettes	melon	onions	yogurt

Ask your teacher or use a picture dictionary to find the meanings of words you don't know.

B2

**The sentences in this recipe are in the wrong order. Listen again and put them in the
correct order.**

A   Fry the chicken in oil or butter
B   Stir the food with a wooden spoon.
C   Add cheese or yogurt, if you like.
D   Add the vegetables to the chicken.
E   Cut up the chicken.
F   Bring the mixture to the boil.
G   Chop the vegetables into small pieces.
H   Put in some pepper and salt.
I   Add half a litre of water to the pan.
J   Fry the chicken and vegetables together.

Does it sound like a good recipe? Could *you* cook this dish? Would you like to?
Why or why not?

C1 You are going to hear somebody ordering a meal in a restaurant. Listen and write down the names of any food or drink you hear.

C2 Listen again and fill in the gaps in the conversation.

WAITER: Would you like to (1) _____ now, madam?

CUSTOMER: Yes, I think I'll have the cream of mushroom (2) _____ to start with,

(3) _____.

WAITER: Cream of (4) _____, right.

CUSTOMER: Then I'll have a green (5) _____, with a (6) _____, I think.

WAITER: (7) _____ do you like it done, madam?

CUSTOMER: Oh, (8) _____, thank you.

WAITER: With chips or new (9) _____?

CUSTOMER: Chips, please. And I'll have the (10) _____ pudding – no, on second

thoughts, the (11) _____ fruit salad afterwards. It's (12) _____!

WAITER: Yes, quite! Now, anything to (13) _____? Some wine, perhaps?

CUSTOMER: No, just a bottle of (14) _____ water, I think.

WAITER: Thank you, madam. And for you, sir?

D SPEAKING PRACTICE

1 Imagine you're in a café, snack bar or restaurant. What would you like to eat? Give your order to the waiter or waitress. With a partner, take turns to be the customer and the waiter.

2 Ask your partner, *'What's your favourite dish in your country? Can you tell me how to make it?'* He or she can ask you, too.

Listening tip

Remember, it isn't always necessary to understand every word when you're listening, so don't panic. Don't think about the words you didn't understand the first time. Relax, and listen again.

4 TICKETS PLEASE!

A **Think about or discuss these questions about travel.**

How often do you travel by train or bus? Do you travel by public transport
a) to go to school or work?   b) on weekend excursions to visit friends or family?
c) when you go on holiday?   d) to go shopping?
Do you prefer travelling by car? Is it cheaper or more convenient than using public transport in your country?

B1 **You are planning to make a train journey soon. You know the route (Gatwick to London), but you would like to make sure there have been no recent changes to the timetable. Listen to the recorded announcement and decide which number you should choose for the information you want.**

Number _____

B2 **Listen again and fill in the missing information.**

Thank you for calling Connex (1) _____ (2) _____.

For general information on (3) _____ availability and fares, please (4) _____ National Rail Enquiries on (5) _____.

Please make (6) _____ selection from the (7) _____ numbers.

Press 1 for a recorded (8) _____ on all Connex trains (9) _____ London.

Press 2 if you have any (10) _____ on the way in (11) _____ we could improve our (12) _____.

Press 3 if you (13) _____ to purchase or (14) _____ a season ticket by (15) _____ card.

Press 4 for (16) _____ other information or if you would like to be (17) _____ to one of our (18) _____ advisers.

Please (19) _____ the number you (20) _____ now.

What happens in your country? Do you phone the station, or a central number, if you want information on trains? Or do you have your own train timetable at home? Can you look up the train timetable on a computer?

What do you think is the best way of finding out this sort of information?

C1 You are going to hear another recorded message, this time for a national coach company. Read the questions, then listen and answer them.

1 Which towns are mentioned?
2 What are the coach stations called?
3 How long does the coach journey between the two places usually take?
4 Does Saturday count as part of the weekend?
5 What is the cheapest possible fare?
6 What number do you phone to book a ticket?

C2 Look at the timetable first. Then listen again and fill in the gaps.

NATIONAL EXPRESS COACHES Monday to Friday		
BRIGHTON	**LONDON**	**BRIGHTON**
Dep 06.00	Arr _____	
Dep _____	Arr 08.40	
	Dep 08.45	Arr _____
Dep _____	Arr 10.40	
Dep every hour on the hour from _____	Arr _____ later	
	Dep every hour on the _____ from 09.30	Arr 1 hour 50 mins later
Saturday and Sunday		
Dep _____	Arr 08.10	
Dep every hour on the hour from _____	Arr 1 hour 50 mins later	
	Dep every hour on the half hour from 10.30	Arr 1 hour 50 mins later
Fares		
<u>Single</u>	<u>Return</u>	<u>Day return</u>
Adult: £6	£_____	£8
Student: £_____	£7.50	£6
Child: £_____	£5	£4
(Child=under 14 Dep=Departs Arr=Arrives)		

D **SPEAKING PRACTICE**

Imagine you are at a railway or bus station ticket office. You want to buy a ticket. Practise your conversation with a partner, using the following conversation to help you.

A: *Hello, I'd like a single/return/day return to Glasgow/London/Manchester, please.*
B: *Right, what time are you travelling?*
A: *I'm going on the 3.20/4.45/7.32/1.54 in ten minutes' time.*
B: *OK, that'll be £5.60/£27.80/£94.63/£13.15, please.*
A: *Here's my Visa card. Can I have a receipt please?*
B: *Right you are. Sign here, please. There's your card and receipt, and your ticket.*
A: *Thank you. Which platform is it?*
B: *Platform number 3/4/5/6/7/8, up the stairs and over the bridge.*
A: *Thanks a lot. Goodbye.*

5 TAKE A MESSAGE

A If you come home and find a message from any of these people on your answerphone, what do you expect to hear? Write down two or three phrases the messages might contain.

1 from a local charity _____

2 from your boss _____

3 from your parents _____

4 from a friend _____

5 from the secretary of a local sports club _____

6 from your doctor's receptionist _____

B1 You are going to hear some messages people left on Sylvia's answerphone while she was away one weekend. Listen and complete the information on Sylvia's notepad.

1 From: Mr Ian Rogers
About: _____
Action to take: ring him to explain
Number: _____

2 From: Mum
About: checking on Sylvia's health
Action to take: _____
Number (mobile): _____

3 From: _____
About: arriving late at work and leaving early
Action to take: _____

4 From: _____
About: charity work
Action to take: ring him back if interested
Number: _____

B2 Listen again and answer the questions.

1 When was Sylvia's appointment?
2 What will happen if she doesn't ring Mr Rogers?
3 Why is Sylvia's mother especially worried about her?
4 Why is Jenny Smith, Sylvia's boss, ringing her at home?
5 Which charity does Edward Fowles work for?
6 Which activities would he like Sylvia to help with?

C1

You are working for a language school one summer, and are helping out at reception. The first thing to do when you arrive at work on Monday morning is to listen to all the messages on the answerphone. Listen and decide whether the statements are true (T) or false (F).

1 Guy Bannister is one of the teachers at the school.
2 He has a visa problem in Moscow.
3 He is arriving on Tuesday.
4 Susanna Fernandez's students have already booked their language course.
5 Her students want to stay for ten weeks.
6 Margareta Svensson is going to miss the first week of her course.
7 She cannot attend because her family are very ill.
8 Barry's car crashed into the school minibus.
9 Fortunately, the minibus is not badly damaged.

C2

Listen again and say how the people giving the messages feel. Choose from the words in the box to describe their feelings.

impatient	very worried	relaxed	sorry	angry

1 Guy _____

2 Susanna _____

3 Margareta _____

4 Barry _____

D

SPEAKING PRACTICE

Write down your own message to a friend, and think what you would say if his/her answerphone is switched on. Make sure you give your name and phone number, and a very clear message. And keep it short! Now say your message to a partner, and ask if the message was clear. Practise again.

Listening tip

Be prepared. Try to think what topics and vocabulary the listening will be about. Before you listen to a recorded message or an answerphone, take a few moments to go through useful vocabulary in your mind. For example, before listening to the answerphone at a language school, you might think of *flight, students, visa, agent, teacher, intensive course, family,* etc. This will help you to understand the message better.

6 THE MISSING DIAMONDS

A Here are some useful words for talking about a crime. Do you know what they mean? Can you add any more words to the list?

motive	suspect	investigate
opportunity	alibi	solve
clues	innocent	solution
evidence	guilty	

B Read the following information carefully.

Lady Paula Prendergast was giving one of her famous dinner parties at her beautiful country house, Pringle Hall. Several close friends were staying there, including her ex-husband Sir Montague Wilberforce, her future husband Derek Donovan, the actor, and Lucy Bisto, a friend of the Honourable Charles Wilberforce, Lady Paula's son. Morgan the butler and Mrs Forbes the housekeeper were also in the house at the time. Suddenly, in the middle of dinner, Lady Paula put her hands to her neck and cried out in horror, 'My diamonds! Where are they? My diamond necklace is missing!' The dinner was left half eaten on the table, as everybody started searching the house for the necklace, but there was no sign of it. It became clear that the necklace, which was worth about half a million pounds, had been lying on the dressing-table in Lady Paula's bedroom between 6 and 7pm. Lady Paula could not remember putting it on for dinner, so it seemed probable that someone had taken it from her bedroom.

B1 Listen to the conversation between the Honourable Charles and Lucy Bisto. Where was everyone between 6 and 7pm? Write each person's name in the correct room, and what he/she was doing.

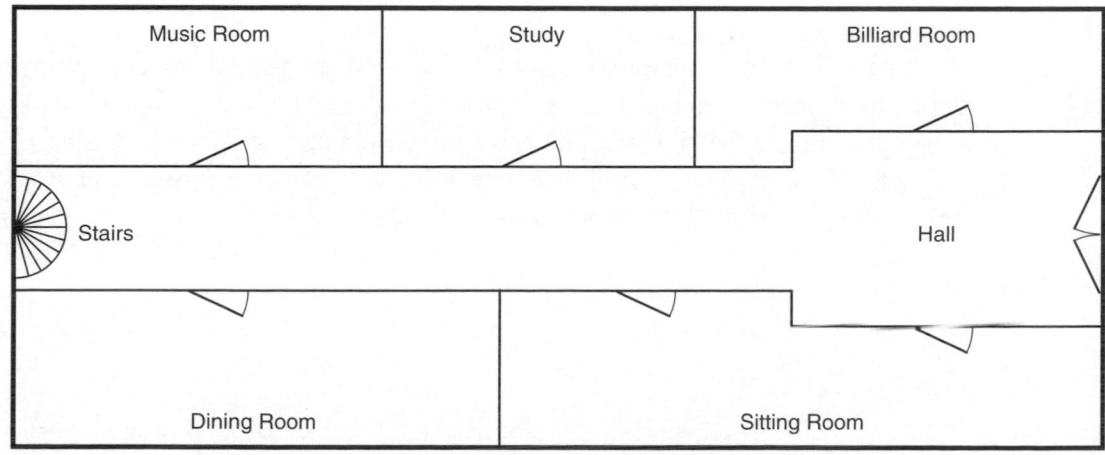

PRINGLE HALL: GROUND FLOOR

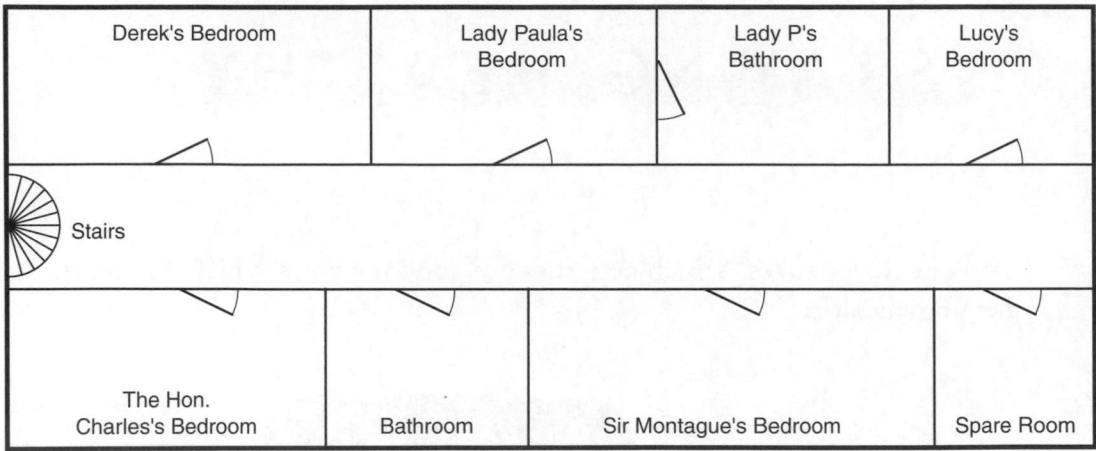

PRINGLE HALL: FIRST FLOOR

Who do you think had *the best opportunity* of stealing the diamonds? Discuss your answers with a partner.

B2   **Now listen to the conversation between Morgan and Mrs Forbes and answer the questions.**

1 Why does Derek want to marry Lady Paula?
2 What does Morgan the butler think about Lady Paula's future marriage to Derek?
3 How does Sir Montague feel about his divorce from Lady Paula?
4 What are his feelings towards Derek Donovan?
5 Why does Lucy hate Lady Paula?
6 Why does Charles need money?
7 What is Mrs Forbes' personal problem?
8 Who do you think has *the best motive* for stealing the diamonds?

Discuss your answers with a partner, and decide who you think the thief was.

Now tell the rest of the class. Be prepared to give your reasons.

C   **PRONUNCIATION PRACTICE:** /ɒ/ /ʌ/ and /e/ /æ/

Watch out for differences in the pronunciation of short vowels. Listen and repeat these words and sentences after the speaker.

1 cot, cut   got, gut   gone, gun   shot, shut   cop, cup   not, nut   choc, chuck

    Have a cup of coffee? With some nuts, or some chocolate?
    Bob lost his job and had to cut his costs.
    Tom shut up shop and chucked the key in a bucket.
    He's got a lot of bottle, but the cops have gone for him with their guns!

2 pet, pat   men, man   Ben, ban   letter, latter   said, sad   met, mat   pen, pan

    The men banned Pat from using her pen.
    The cat sat on the mat and Ben penned a letter.
    Ben patted his pet and said sadly, 'I've never met a cat like you!'

7 STAYING HEALTHY

A Look at the pictures. Which activities are good for you? Which do you think could be bad for your health?

A   B   C

D   E   F

B1 You are going to hear five young people talking about exercise, fitness and general health. Listen and match the speakers 1–5 to the pictures above. There is one extra picture.

B2 Read the statements, then listen again and choose one correct statement for each speaker. There are two extra statements.

Speaker 1	A ... has tried to give something up.
Speaker 2	B ... hates exercise.
Speaker 3	C ... plays and watches a sport.
Speaker 4	D ... takes exercise every day.
Speaker 5	E ... is fitter now than last year.
	F ... only exercises at weekends.
	G ... enjoys exercising with friends.

Why do people take exercise?

What kind of exercise do you take, and how often? Do you think you should take more, or less?

What is the best kind of exercise, do you think?

What kind of foods are good or bad for you? Make a list, and see if other students agree with you.

C1

You are going to hear a doctor talking on a radio programme. She is giving some advice on staying fit and healthy. Look at the words in the box, then listen and tick (✔) the ones that you hear.

bread	energy	meals	tennis
cheese	exercise	salt	vegetables
coffee	football	stress	vitamins
diet	fruit	tea	wine

C2

Listen again and tick (✔) the correct sentences.

1 Breakfast is not an important meal.
2 We should eat a large lunch.
3 It's necessary to put a little salt in food while it is cooking.
4 Drink as much tea and coffee as you like.
5 We should eat different kinds of food.
6 Everybody needs the same amount of exercise.
7 Aerobics is a better type of exercise than swimming.
8 It's important to choose a type of exercise that you like.
9 You can save money by taking exercise.
10 You can phone Dr O'Neill tomorrow to ask about stress.

D

SPEAKING PRACTICE

Do you agree with Dr O'Neill's ideas?
How do *you* keep fit?
How often are you ill?
How much exercise do you take every week?
How much water do you drink every day?

Find out what other students' answers to these questions are.

Listening tip

Don't be afraid to ask the speaker to repeat or explain what s/he said, as Ryan did in the interview. If you don't understand when you're listening, say:
I'm sorry, I didn't quite catch what you said about ...
Sorry to interrupt, but ...
Could I just ask ...
Did you say ... or ...?
Sorry, what was that?
What did you say your name was?
Sorry?   Pardon?
Make sure your voice goes up at the end of your question.

8 HOW DO YOU SAY...?

A

When speaking or writing to people we don't know well, we usually use formal language. With other people, we use informal language. Decide whether these expressions are formal (F) or informal (I).

Sorry I forgot ...
I am extremely grateful.
Bye, see you later.
I do apologise.
Here, take this.
Hi there!

Please accept this.
I hope that you have an enjoyable time.
Have fun!
Thanks a lot.
How do you do?
My regards to your parents. Goodbye.

Now find expressions from the list above (one formal and one informal) which have a similar meaning, to make six pairs.

B1

You are going to hear five speakers, using formal and informal language. Read the statements, then listen and choose the correct statement for each speaker. There are three extra statements.

Speaker 1
Speaker 2
Speaker 3
Speaker 4
Speaker 5

A ... is leaving his/her job.
B ... has photocopied the wrong report.
C ... has forgotten to book some tickets.
D ... is asking for advice.
E ... is giving a talk.
F ... wants to change some concert tickets.
G ... thinks someone isn't doing his/her job properly.
H ... has not met this person before.

B2

Listen to the tone of voice this time, as well as the words, and match each speaker to the correct feeling. There are three extra feelings.

Speaker 1
Speaker 2
Speaker 3
Speaker 4
Speaker 5

A bored
B miserable
C angry
D tired
E pleased
F grateful
G sorry
H hopeful

C1

You are going to hear a student talking about the languages that he speaks. Listen and tick (✔) the correct information.

1 Fluent languages: Malay   Chinese   Arabic   English   German

2 Father's nationality: English   German   Chinese   Malaysian

3 Mother's nationality: Chinese   Italian   English   Egyptian

4 Speaks a little: German   Italian   English   Arabic

5 Best at speaking: English   Arabic   Malay   Chinese

6 Best at writing: Arabic   English   German   Chinese   Malay

7 Wants to improve: Chinese   English   German   Arabic

C2

Listen again and match the two halves of the sentences.

1 He speaks Malay   A which is the capital of Malaysia.
2 He speaks Mandarin Chinese   B because he was sent to an English school.
3 He speaks English   C to improve his languages.
4 He lives in Kuala Lumpur,   D because his father's Malaysian.
5 He speaks Chinese with his friends, E because his mother's Chinese.
6 His main problem is listening,   F so that's his favourite language.
7 He'd like to travel abroad   G because people speak so fast.

D

PRONUNCIATION PRACTICE: Contractions

We often run words together, or shorten them, so it's sometimes difficult to hear all the words in a sentence. Listen to the six sentences and write down the number of words in them. A contraction (like *I've, he's, isn't*) counts as two words.

1 _____   2 _____   3 _____   4 _____   5 _____   6 _____

Listen and repeat these forms after the speaker:

she's   I've   haven't   isn't   we're   here's   you'll

Listen to the six sentences again and repeat after the speaker.

Listening tip

English sounds in slow, formal speech may sound quite different in informal conversations, or when people speak fast. Look out for these contractions:

I'd (= I had/I would)   *he's* (= he has/he is)
isn't (= is not)   *doesn't* (= does not)
can't (= cannot)   *aren't* (= are not)
won't (= will not)   *shan't* (= shall not)

9 FLYING HIGH

A   **What is happening in the picture? What words or phrases do you hear or use when talking about flights? Match the questions to the answers.**

1   *Which gate number is it?*
2   *How early do we have to check in?*
3   *Is it a scheduled or charter flight?*
4   *How much hand luggage can I take with me?*
5   *Is there a reduction for children?*
6   *Can I have a window seat?*

A   *Only one bag, I'm afraid.*
B   *Scheduled – it goes daily.*
C   *Yes, 50%.*
D   *Number 24.*
E   *Sorry, they've all been taken.*
F   *Two hours before departure.*

Which of questions 1–6 are probably asked at the travel agent's, and which at the airport check-in desk?

B1   **You are going to hear four people asking for or giving information about flying. Read the statements, then listen and choose the correct statement for each speaker. There are two extra statements.**

Speaker 1	A ... is checking in at the airport.	D ... is confirming flight details.
Speaker 2	B ... is making a complaint.	E ... is changing a flight.
Speaker 3	C ... is asking for information.	F ... is booking a flight.
Speaker 4		

B2   **Read the statements, then listen again and decide whether they are true (T) or false (F).**

1   The first speaker wants to spend a week in Canada.
2   The charter flight to Toronto costs £450.
3   The second speaker is extremely worried about possible delays.
4   Her flight leaves Corfu at 03.23 on Saturday 25th.
5   The third speaker has only got hand luggage.
6   He'd prefer a no-smoking seat.
7   The fourth speaker plans to travel alone.
8   She is booking only just in time.

C1 You are going to hear some airport announcements. You are travelling to Pisa and your friend is travelling to Madrid, so listen carefully for information about both of these flights. Answer the questions.

1 Which gate should you go to?
2 What time will your flight depart?
3 Which gate should your friend go to?
4 What time will her flight depart?

C2 Listen again and complete the information.

FLIGHT NUMBER	DESTINATION	DEPARTURE TIME	GATE	ADVICE
BA2724	STOCKHOLM			BOARDING
EAF3310		10.22	32	BOARDING
AF8728	RIGA		11	
KGC934		11.05		BOARDING
	LISBON	11.10		
CA5541		11.25		WAIT IN LOUNGE
	BONN			WAIT IN LOUNGE

D SPEAKING PRACTICE

Practise these situations with a partner.

1 You are asking for information at a travel agent's, because you're planning next year's holiday.
2 You are booking a flight in person or by phone.
3 You are checking in at the airline desk at the airport, at the start of your holiday.
4 You are confirming flight details for the return trip to your country after your holiday.

Listening tip   Remember that English is spoken by people all round the world, so it's good for you to listen to as many different accents as possible.

10 OUT AND ABOUT

A

Match the words on the left to the words on the right. They all have something to do with entertainment. Use each word once only.

1	film	A	dancer
2	stage	B	singer
3	opera	C	theatre
4	novel	D	reading
5	ballet	E	television
6	quiz show	F	cinema

What are your favourite kinds of entertainment? How often do you go out in the evening? Do you prefer going out alone, with one or two special friends, or with a large group of friends?

B1

You are going to hear a recorded theatre announcement. Look at the words in the box and predict the ones you do NOT expect to hear. Then listen and tick (✔) the words that you hear.

actor	director	musical	reviews
box office	evening	performance	stage
cartoon	film	play	theatre
comedy	matinee	prices	tickets

B2

Listen again and complete the information.

THE GRAND THEATRE, WEXHAM

This week, the Royal Shakespeare (1) _____ in A MIDSUMMER NIGHT'S DREAM by William Shakespeare, from (2) _____ to Saturday. (3) _____ performances at 2.30pm on (4) _____ and Saturday. Evening performances at (5) _____.

Prices from (6) _____ to £22. Next week, for (7) _____ nights only, the (8) _____ London Theatre in A WOMAN IN WHITE, starting at 8pm on (9) _____, Thursday and (10) _____. Prices from £7 to (11) _____.

To book tickets, press (12) _____ on your phone and have your (13) _____ card ready, or ring the (14) _____ office on 01752 (15) _____ .

C1

You are going to hear three young people discussing plans for this evening. Listen and match two of the statements to each speaker.

Harry	A	... accepts the invitation to the cinema.
Adam	B	... dislikes horror films.
Ellie	C	... suggests going to the cinema.
	D	... has seen one film several times.
	E	... enjoys Woody Allen films.
	F	... would prefer a horror film.

C2

Listen again and write down the exact words of the answers to these questions. (Contractions like *he's* count as two words.)

1 Hi Adam, do you fancy seeing a film tonight?

(4 words) _____

2 What do you think, Harry?

(6 words) _____

3 How about it, Ellie?

(5 words) _____

4 Isn't there *any*thing we can agree on?

(9 words) _____

D

SPEAKING PRACTICE

Here are some useful ways of accepting or refusing invitations.

Yes, let's. Great idea!   Yes, why not? What's on?   Yes, I'd love to.
Sorry, I've got something else on.   I am sorry, I'm afraid I'm busy.

Practise these situations with a partner.

1 You invite a friend to a rock concert, but s/he has something else planned for that date.
2 You ask someone at work to play squash with you, and s/he likes the idea.
3 You invite your best friend to the cinema tonight, and s/he accepts.
4 You ask someone you don't know well to the theatre. Unfortunately, s/he can't come.

Listening tip

A good way of practising listening is to video English-language films. You can replay them again and again until you understand them really well. Don't worry about words you don't know, just concentrate on the general meaning.

11 HOME SWEET HOME

A **Think about or discuss these questions about homes.**

Where would you like to live? In your family home, or in a student hostel?
Would you prefer to live alone, in a flat, or in a room in someone's house? Or you could
share a flat or a house with your friends or other students.
Which would be   a) cheaper?   b) more fun?   c) better for studying?

B1 **You are going to hear a phone conversation between the owner of a flat and someone who
wants to rent a place to live. Read the questions, then listen and answer them.**

1   Who is making the phone call, the man or the woman?
2   What is the woman a bit worried about?
3   Who does most of the talking, the man or the woman, and why?

B2 Here is Julia's notepad. Listen again
and fill in the information she wants
with *Yes*, *No*, or a different answer.

> Ring Mr Cage about that flat
> Address? _____ Edward Road
> Self-contained? _____
> Large? _____
> Warm? _____
> Any special advantages?
> _____
> How much per week? _____
> Are bills included? _____
> Go and see it tonight? _____
> What time? _____

What are the advantages and disadvantages of this flat? Do you think Julia will rent it?
What would *you* do in her situation?

C1   You are going to hear Grant and his wife, Sharon, talking about doing some work on their house. Listen and write down the names of the four rooms that they are discussing. They don't name the room that they are in, so you will have to think about this.

C2   Read the sentences, then listen again and match the speakers to the sentences that you hear them say. Use G for Grant and S for Sharon. If Sharon and Grant agree, use B for both.

1   The place still looks a mess.   ☐

2   Where do you think we should start?   ☐

3   We should throw away that horrible old brown carpet, too.   ☐

4   I hate those pink walls!   ☐

5   The shower's not working properly.   ☐

6   Look how dirty these walls are!   ☐

7   It really needs some new wallpaper.   ☐

8   We can't do all this ourselves.   ☐

D   **PRONUNCIATION PRACTICE:**   /tʃ/ /ʃ/ and /θ/ /ð/ /s/

1   Can you hear the difference between these pairs of words? *Ch* is a much harder sound than *sh*. Listen and repeat the words and sentences after the speaker.

chair, share   watch, wash   cheese, she's   choose, shoes   catch, cash
match, mash   chip, ship   cheap, sheep

Watch out! You'll fall off that chair!
Is she really choosing those shoes?
Shall we share the cash, and watch the match?

2   Here is another group of similar-sounding words. To produce a correct *th* sound, your tongue should be between your teeth. Listen and repeat the words and sentences after the speaker.

thick, sick   worth, worse   think, sink   thumb, some   mouth, mouse
although, also   that, sat

This fog is so thick – it's worse than I thought!
The child put her thumb rather thoughtfully into her mouth.
They sat there, thinking beautiful thoughts about something.

> *Listening tip*
>
> In Grant and Sharon's conversation you can hear some of the 100 most frequently used words in English, for example, *we, to, think, about, a, of, this, do, you, in, and, the, is*. Most conversations are made up of these very short, simple words that you can easily recognise. If you remember this, perhaps it will make you more confident when listening.

12 PHONING AND FOLLOWING INSTRUCTIONS

A Match the conversations to the responses in the box.

1 'Is that 887491?'   'No, it's 887492.'
2 'Is Penny there?'   'No, I'm sorry, she's out.'
3 'Mike Barton speaking.'   'Hello, can you switch your fax on, please?'
4 'Hello, can I speak to Simon?'   'Oh, he doesn't live here any more.'
5 'Is Mr Hodge there, please?'   'I'm afraid he's on holiday this week.'

A 'OK, I'll ring back next week then.'		D 'Of course, right away.'
B 'Could you give her a message, please?'		E 'Do you know his new address?'
C 'Oh, sorry, wrong number.'		

B1 You are going to hear three phone conversations. Listen and match the conversations to the descriptions. There is one extra description.

Conversation 1   A a parent asking for help
Conversation 2   B a customer making a complaint
Conversation 3   C a friend giving some news
                      D a driver speaking to a policeman

How do you think the people making the phone calls feel? Choose one adjective from the box for each conversation.

tired	sad	angry	delighted	shocked	worried

B2 Listen again and complete the sentences with ONE word in each gap.

1 The customer has a _____ with the _____ she bought _____.

2 Nothing _____ when she switches it _____.

3 The store will refund her _____, if she takes it back with the _____.

4 Janet has got a new _____.

5 She's going to live in _____.

6 Mrs Jenkins can't _____ where her daughter is.

7 She set out to meet her _____ at _____ o'clock.

8 Her usual _____ for coming home is _____ o'clock.

C1 You are going to hear four people giving instructions on how to use something. Listen and match the speakers 1–4 to the pictures.

A   B   C   D

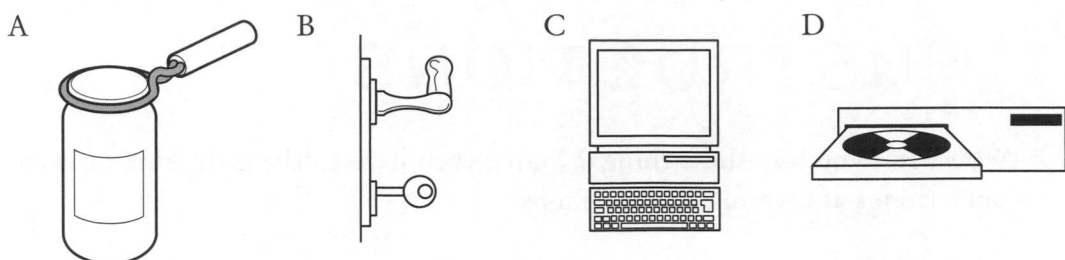

C2 Listen again and choose the correct word or phrase you hear from the pair in each box.

Speaker 1   sticky / tricky   idea / ID   the locket / to lock it

push down / pull down

Speaker 2   properly / probably   getting start it / getting started   festival / first of all

on the keeper / on the keyboard

Speaker 3   what I do / what I'd do   button here / bottom here   disk in / desk in

Speaker 4   really well / really will   one end of the rubber / one end of the robber

holding the hand / holding the handle

C3 Listen again and choose the right information or opinion from the box for each speaker.

A It's fun to use.	C It's difficult at first.
B It's a good way of solving a problem.	D There's a lot to learn.

D SPEAKING PRACTICE

When you answer the phone in English, you give your name or phone number, or say what your company likes you to say. For example:

Richard speaking.   Richard here.   Richard Smith speaking.
Good morning, Bates and Lunn, Anna speaking. How may I help you?
Essex Arts Club, Steve here. Can I help you?

Here are some more useful expressions to use on the phone:

I'm afraid he's in a meeting.   Could I leave a message?
Just a moment, I'll see if she's in.   Could you ask her to ring me back?
Can I take a message?   Thanks for your help.

Practise phone conversations with a partner.

13 SHOPPING

A

Where can you buy these things? Match each item to the right kind of shop. (You can buy some things at several different shops.)

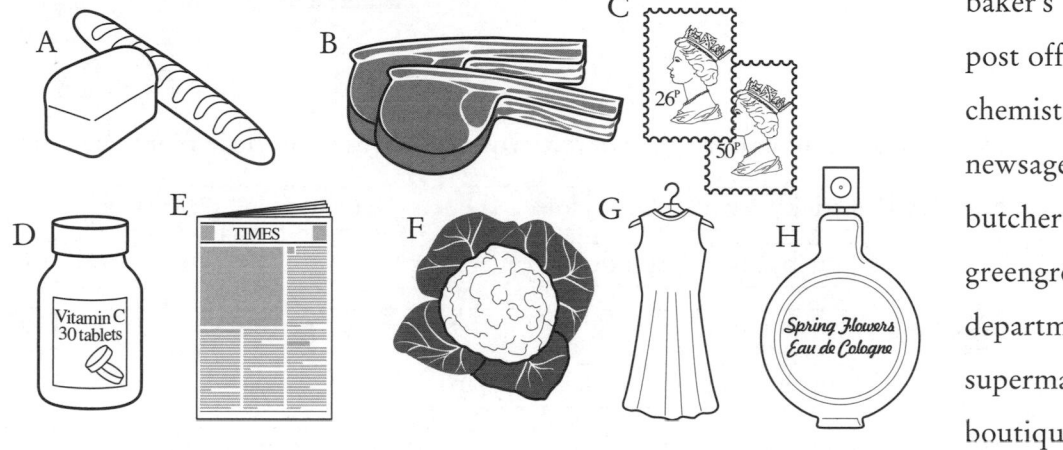

baker's

post office

chemist's

newsagent's

butcher's

greengrocer's

department store

supermarket

boutique

Do you prefer buying food in small shops or at supermarkets? How often do you go shopping for food or clothes?

B1

You are going to hear a conversation between Zoë and George, who are planning to have a picnic with some friends. Listen and tick (✔) all the items that they are going to buy.

beef	fruit juice	peaches
bread	lemonade	potatoes
butter	lettuce	radishes
carrots	mayonnaise	salad dressing
cheese	milk	strawberries
chicken	oil	tomatoes
crisps	olives	tuna
cucumber	onions	white wine
eggs	pasta	

B2

Listen again and complete the sentences from the conversation.

1 OK, that's great! Now _____ list?

2 Oh yes! _____ a tin of tuna?

3 What _____ need? Oh yes, the drinks.

4 And lots and lots of strawberries – _____!

What do you think of George and Zoë's plans for the picnic?

C1 Listen to the man's story and answer the questions by ticking the correct answer.

1 What was the first present the man bought for his girlfriend?

A    B 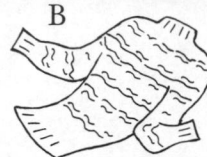   C 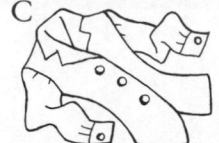   D

2 Where did he buy it?

A    B    C

3 What did he change it for?

A    B 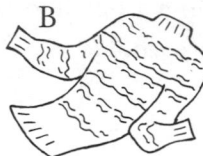   C 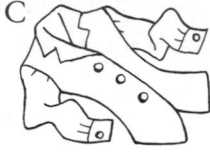   D

4 Where did the second girl in the story live?
A in the next house
B in the flat above the man
C in the house opposite
D in the next street

C2 Listen again and tick (✔) the correct sentences.

1 He went to more than one shop to choose the present.
2 He knew his girlfriend disliked red.
3 He wasn't sure of his girlfriend's size.
4 He gave the blouse to the girl next door because she liked it.
5 His girlfriend didn't mind seeing the girl next door wearing the green blouse.

D SPEAKING PRACTICE

Here are some useful expressions to use when shopping for clothes.

SHOP ASSISTANT: *Good morning, can I help you?*
CUSTOMER: *Yes, have you got any swimsuits in stock?*   *How much is this jacket?*
I'd like a scarf/a pair of socks/some tights, please.
Can I try on this suit, please?   *Are there any other colours?*
I think I need a bigger/smaller size.
Have you got this in a size 38, please?
Yes, I'll take it. Can I pay by credit card?

Practise conversations with a partner; one person is the customer, the other is the shop assistant.

14 IT'S A SMALL WORLD

A **Think about or discuss these questions.**

Have you ever met someone you know in a strange place, completely unexpectedly?
Why do people say 'It's a small world?' Do you agree or not?

Have you ever visited the United States? If so, which places did you visit? If not, where would you like to go?

B1 **You are going to hear a woman telling a story about her trip to the USA. Look at the map, then listen and mark the route that she took.**

B2 **Read the questions, then listen again and answer them.**

1 How long ago did the woman's story happen?
2 Why did she go to the USA?
3 How long did she stay in New York?
4 How did she travel around the country?
5 What part of her trip did she enjoy most?
6 Where did she meet her brother?
7 Why was it a surprise?
8 Why was it lucky for him?

C1 You are going to hear another traveller talking about a recent holiday that he had with his wife in India. Read the statements, then listen and tick (✔) the correct ones.

1 It was an expensive holiday.
2 They want to get all their money back.
3 The holiday lasted for two weeks.
4 They stayed in a 5-star hotel.
5 They were expecting to get three meals a day.
6 There were some good points about the holiday.

C2 Listen again and complete the notes the man made during his holiday.

<u>Holiday in India</u>

With _____ company

Hotel name: **the Shelton (Hyderabad)**

Number of days: _____

Total cost: _____

<u>Problems</u>

Room: a)_____ b)_____

Food: a)_____ b)_____

Service: _____

Waiters: _____

Excursions: a)_____ b)_____

Action to take: **Get some of our money back!**

D PRONUNCIATION PRACTICE: Short and long vowels

Listen and repeat these words after the speaker.

sit, seat	dip, deep	hill, heal	chip, cheap	hit, heat	fill, feel	wick, weak
got, goat	rod, road	Tod, toad	doll, dole	mop, mope	hop, hope	
fat, fate	hat, hate	mac, make	back, bake	sack, sake	rack, rake	
lit, light	bit, bite	mitt, might	hit, height	Brit, bright	sit, sight	

15 MEETING AND GREETING

A

What words do you use when you meet people or when you say goodbye? Match each picture to one of the speech bubbles. There is one extra speech bubble.

A   B

C   D

1 So sorry I'm late – I got stuck in a traffic jam!

2 I'll give you a ring very soon – OK?

3 No, no, it's my turn to pay!

4 Come and stay with us any time – my parents would love to see you.

5 Jack, do you know Nathan Oliver? Jack Bennett, Nathan Oliver.

B1

You are going to hear four short conversations. Read the statements, then listen and decide whether they are true (T) or false (F).

1 Joshua and Megan haven't seen each other for years.
2 Joshua now lives in Seattle.
3 Nathan Oliver has worked for the company longer than Jack Bennett.
4 Jack Bennett has an interesting idea for Nathan Oliver.
5 Emma was travelling by bus to meet her friend.
6 Rebecca got wet because she had to walk there.
7 Emma and Rebecca were planning to go to the theatre.
8 The two men have just had a meal.
9 They are brothers.

B2

Listen again and decide how the people sound. Choose TWO adjectives each time.

1 The woman: interested   busy   sociable
  The man: forgetful   in a hurry   friendly

2 The woman: in control   positive   tired
  The new assistant: business-like   polite   unsure

3 First girl: surprised   cross   sorry
  Second girl: sad   angry   critical

4 The two men: relaxed   generous   hungry

C1

You are going to hear two people meeting at a party. Listen and tick (✔) the words that you hear.

chocolate	hobbies	jobs	life	smell
company	home	lab	news	taste
friend	jackets	leather	scientist	work

C2

Listen again and choose from A, B or C to complete the sentences correctly.

1 Charlie and Rachel A are friends.
                                     B work in the same office.
                                     C have just met for the first time.

2 Charlie works A for Gucci.
                     B with Annette.
                     C for Prada.

3 Charlie A buys jackets.
              B buys leather.
              C wears leather jackets.

4 Rachel works A in a lab.
                   B in a kitchen.
                   C at a chemist's.

5 Rachel A makes chocolate.
            B enjoys eating chocolate.
            C tastes chocolate.

D

PRONUNCIATION PRACTICE: Chunking

When you listen to English, you hear people pausing between groups of words or sounds (sometimes called 'chunks'). A pause often shows that there's going to be a change in meaning, or a new idea, or some extra information. Listen to these sentences from Exercise C, and mark where you hear a pause.

1 Yes I used to work with her actually at Prada.
2 Oh really what do you do?
3 Well actually I used to love chocolate.
4 Let me get you another drink tomato juice was it?

Listen and repeat the sentences after the speaker, pausing in the correct places.

Listening tip

If you are listening to a tape, concentrate on the most important facts the first time you listen. Think about the background, and imagine yourself in that situation. Then, when you listen for the second or third time, you will be able to catch the details.

16 THE QUEEN'S HOUSE

A

Think about or discuss these questions about visiting old buildings.

What kind of information would you want to find out if you visited an old house where people lived hundreds of years ago?

What words would you expect to hear from a tour guide in an old house or palace?

B1

Look at the floor plan of the Queen's House in Greenwich, and the list of rooms. Listen to the guided tour of the house and fill in the names of the rooms on the plan.

King's Stateroom	Queen's Stateroom
King's Waiting Room	Queen's Waiting Room
King's Bedroom	Queen's Bedroom
Music Room	Dining Room
Library	Study
King's Bathroom	Maid's Room

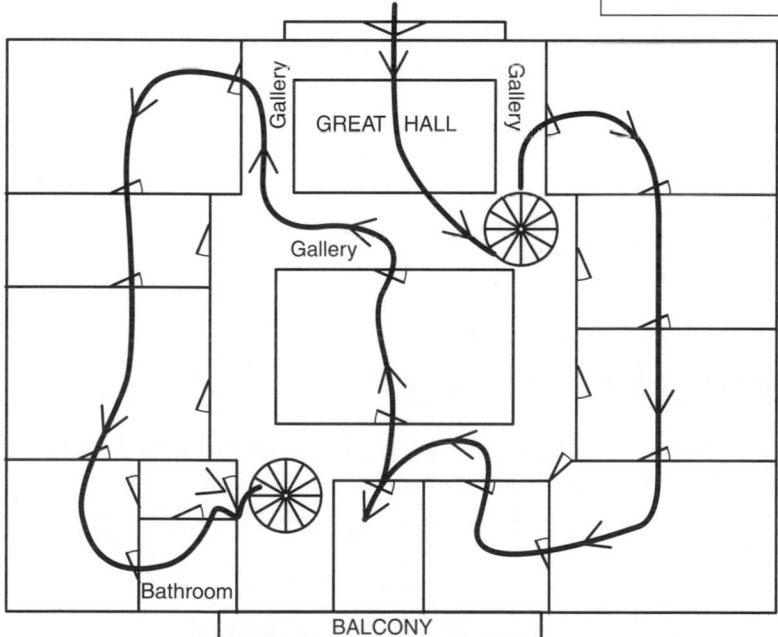

B2

Listen again and answer the questions. Choose the correct answer (A, B or C).

1 Where is the Queen's House?
   A in Denmark   B in Italy   C in London

2 Who did the house first belong to?
   A Inigo Jones   B Anne of Denmark   C Charles I

3 The house was built between
   A 1616 and 1635.   B 1635 and 1716.   C 1660 and 1735.

4 The black and white marble floor is in
   A the Gallery.   B the Great Hall.   C the King's Bathroom.

5 Which is the 'most richly-furnished' room in the house?
   A the King's Stateroom   B the Great Hall   C the King's Waiting-room
6 Which room is just like the King's Bedroom?
   A the King's Stateroom   B the Bathroom   C the Queen's Bedroom

C1 You are going to hear a conversation between a couple who have just visited the Queen's House. Listen and tick (✔) the words that you hear.

boat trip	cheap	cost	restaurant	tea
bus	chips	market	shopping	visit
café	coach trip	museum	taxi	visitor

C2 Listen again and complete the sentences from the conversation.

1 Now, what shall we _____ next?

2 I'm not going anywhere. My _____.

3 How about _____ on the River Thames?

4 You spend _____ at home.

5 How much _____?

6 They do a lovely _____ in the National Gallery restaurant.

7 But I warn you, next year _____ home.

8 You can _____ on your own!

D **PRONUNCIATION PRACTICE: / h / and -*ough***

1 Listen and repeat these words after the speaker, making sure you pronounce the *h* sound.

hello   hair   Harry   his   hers   happy   hurry   horse   haunted   house

Harry's on holiday in Honolulu in a haunted house.
Have you heard, horse-riding makes Helen happy?

2 -*ough* is a difficult sound in English, because there are several different ways of pronouncing it. Listen and repeat after the speaker.

rough, tough, enough
thorough, borough
thought, bought, sought, fought
cough   through

I thought I'd bought a tough pair of shoes.
She coughed all through the night.
It's a rough borough to live in.

17 FREE TIME

A

What are your spare-time interests and how much time do you spend on them? Match the pictures to five of these activities.

rock climbing	reading	going to the cinema
parachuting	driving fast cars	birdwatching
sailing	travelling	

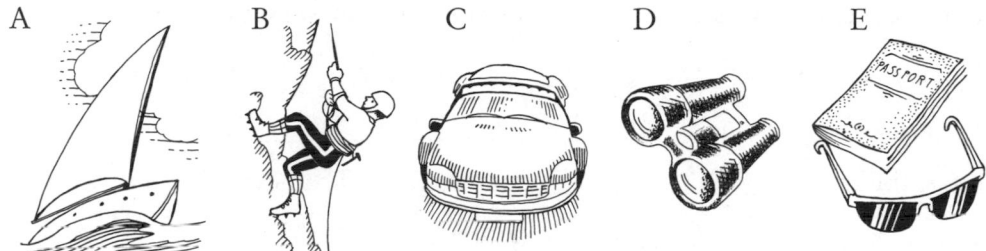

A   B   C   D   E

B1

You are going to hear a recorded message, giving information about summer study courses in a country house. Listen and number the courses in the order that you hear them mentioned.

Family History	Intensive Russian	Writing Short Stories
Intensive French	Modern Art	Yoga
Intensive Japanese	Tennis	
Intensive Portuguese	Understanding the Internet	

B2

Read the statements, then listen again and decide whether they are true (T) or false (F).

At Little Stoke Manor this summer ...

1 ... the new programme starts next week.
2 ... you can study Portuguese and French at the same time.
3 ... David Malcolm will teach for two weeks.
4 ... you can practise tennis in a group.
5 ... Lizzie Windrush will talk about family history.
6 ... yoga is a new course.
7 ... yoga is available only at weekends.
8 ... Peter Dennis is the computer expert.
9 ... you can study Modern Art in June.
10 ... you should ring 0191 48765 to book.

C1

You are going to hear two friends, Scott and Melissa, discussing fitness centres in their area. Listen and complete the information in the table.

Name	What's available	Price	Where	Phone number
1 Sweatshop	_____ weights	_____	Town centre	_____
2 _____	gym, _____ yoga	£180 a year	Near station	_____
3 _____	_____, sauna _____, aerobics free car park	_____	Out of town	

C2

Listen again and choose the exact words (A, B, C or D) used by the speakers.

1 A That's a good price, isn't it?
   B That's cheap, isn't it?
   C That's very reasonable.
   D This isn't very expensive.

2 A What's on offer there?
   B What facilities has it got?
   C What's available there?
   D What equipment has it got?

3 A You could travel by train.
   B You could take the train.
   C You could come in on the train.
   D You could arrive by train.

4 A Maybe this one's worth a look.
   B This one may be OK.
   C Maybe this one is suitable.
   D This one may be what we want.

D

SPEAKING PRACTICE

People often ask and answer questions about their hobbies like this.

A: *What do you do in your spare time?*   B: *Well, I like computer games and ...*
A: *Do you belong to any clubs?*   B: *Yes, I'm a member of my local swimming club.*
A: *How long have you been interested in old clocks?*   B: *For about the last three years.*
A: *How often do you watch football?*   B: *Whenever I have time, about once a week.*

With a partner, practise conversations like these about your own hobbies.

Listening tip

Use your hobbies and spare-time activities to practise your listening. If you like pop music, for example, try writing down the words of any of your favourite songs. If you like the cinema, watch out for films in English. If you like listening to the radio or watching TV, tune into English-language channels, like the BBC or CNN.

18 DANGER!

A

Match the words in the box to their meanings. You are going to hear them in Part B, so you need to know what they mean.

1. when a boat turns over in the water
2. a large sailing boat
3. the floor of a boat
4. when there are a lot of waves
5. a large ship for people, cars and lorries, taking the same route regularly
6. a kind of waistcoat with air in it, that you should wear when sailing, to keep you up if you fall into the water

life-jacket	yacht
deck	capsize
ferry	rough sea

B1

Listen to Sam's story and put the pictures in the right order.

B2

Listen again and decide whether the sentences are true (T) or false (F).

1. Sam has never had a more dangerous experience.
2. Alice knows his yacht.
3. This all happened last summer.
4. He was sailing from North Wales to Northern Ireland.
5. There were four men on the boat.
6. Only two of them were wearing life-jackets.
7. They all sat on top of the capsized boat.
8. The ferry changed its route in order to pick them up.

Mark on the map where you think the accident happened.

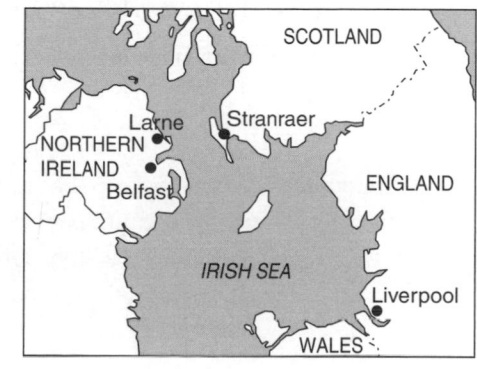

C1 You are going to hear two people talking about a trip to New Zealand. Look at the pictures, then listen and tick (✔) the things that they mention.

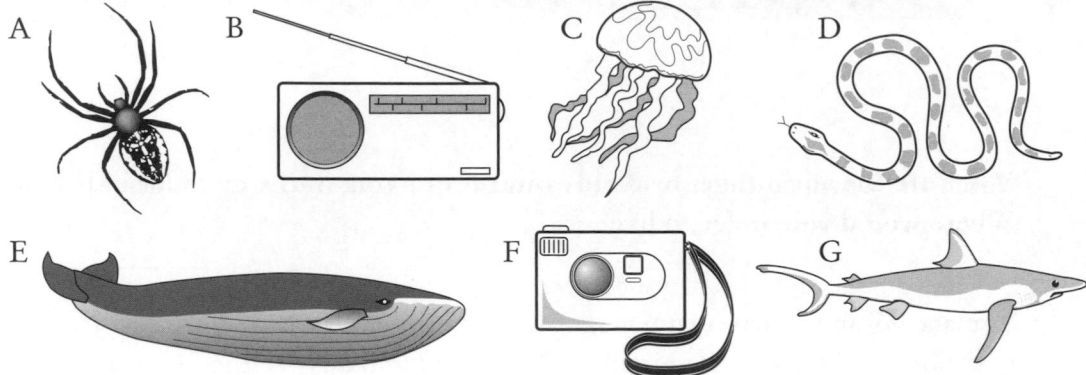

A   B   C   D

E   F   G

C2 Read the 'Possible danger' column, then listen again and complete the 'Action to take' column.

Possible danger	Action to take
1 You meet a shark when diving in the sea.	The best thing to do is … _____
2 You see a jellyfish close to you when you're swimming.	It's a good thing to … _____
3 A small black spider with a red patch bites you.	You'll have to … _____
4 You're travelling with all your luggage in your car. You want to park and walk along the beach.	You shouldn't … _____

D PRONUNCIATION PRACTICE: Falling intonation and sentence stress

Most sentences in English end with a falling tone, when your voice goes *down* at the end. Listen and repeat after the speaker.

1 I'd never been there.
2 It's later than I thought.
3 They've planted two apple trees.
4 The flight takes five hours.
5 We'll have to pay the bills this week.
6 She's bought a cottage in the country.
7 You'll always be welcome.
8 She's a very good writer.
9 What a lovely day!
10 He often arrives late.

Now underline the words where you think there is a strong stress. Listen again and repeat after the speaker, making sure that you use correct stress *and* bring your voice down at the end of each sentence.

19 TOWN AND COUNTRY

A What are the advantages or disadvantages of living in the town, or in the country? Where would *you* prefer to live?

B1 You are going to hear a conversation between two women, Amy and Jessica. Read the questions and look at the pictures, then listen and answer the questions by ticking (✔) the right pictures.

1 What kind of job does Amy do?

A  B C

2 Where does Jessica work?

A  B C

3 Why does Amy think roads are sometimes dangerous in the country?

A  B  C

B2 Read the questions, then listen again and answer them.

1 Does Jessica know Amy well or not? How do you know?
2 What exactly is Amy's job?
3 Why do farmers need her?
4 How does Jessica feel about Amy's job?
5 What nearly happened to Amy this morning?
6 What does Amy like about working in the country?

C1

Listen to this conversation between Rory and Patsy and decide whether the statements are true (T) or false (F).

1 Rory and Patsy went to the theatre together.
2 The theatre opened recently.
3 Rory saw the play at the Edinburgh Festival.
4 The last bus to Winterbourne leaves at 11 p.m.
5 Rory enjoyed the busy atmosphere on the streets.
6 He went to Café Prague by taxi.
7 He thinks the evening was too expensive.

C2

Listen again and complete Patsy's questions or comments.

1 Hi Rory! Did you _____?

2 Oh. Where _____?

3 How long's _____?

4 Oh brilliant! Did you go _____?

5 I bet that _____.

6 You should _____!

D

PRONUNCIATION PRACTICE: Rising and falling intonation

English speakers usually make their voices go up at the end of a sentence if they are asking a question and expecting a *Yes/No* answer. Listen and repeat these questions after the speaker, with a rising intonation.

1 Are you sure it's number 2?
2 Did you lock the door?
3 Is there a shop that sells milk?
4 Do *you* always walk the dog?
5 Do you live near the school?
6 Has he lived there for long?
7 Are you on holiday next week?
8 Is it the first today?
9 Did they come by bus?
10 Have you seen the doctor yet?

Now look at these questions and decide whether your voice should rise (if it's a *Yes/No* question) or fall (if it asks for information). Mark them UP or DOWN at the end of the sentence. Listen and check.

11 How are you today?
12 Can you swim?
13 What's your name?
14 Have you got a bike?
15 Where does she live?
16 Why are you late?
17 Have you got any pets?
18 Do you speak Arabic?
19 How much did that cost?
20 Do you like him?

Listen again and repeat numbers 11–20 after the speaker.

20 SCHOOL AND COLLEGE

A **Think about or discuss these questions about education.**

What age do children start school and leave school in your country?
Which do you think is better, a state school or a private school, and why?
Is it a good idea to study at college/university?
Do you think university students work hard or not?

B1 **You are going to hear five people talking about school, or about their work or studies.**
Listen and tick (✔) the words that you hear.

break	freedom	lunches	science	teacher
children	games	money	stories	timetable
exams	lessons	pupils	studying	uniforms

B2 **Listen again and match the speakers to the correct information. There are two extra pieces of information.**

Speaker 1	A ... is still a school pupil.
Speaker 2	B ... no longer works as a teacher.
Speaker 3	C ... works as a school cleaner.
Speaker 4	D ... teaches part-time.
Speaker 5	E ... really liked his/her school.
	F ... is a university student.
	G ... has children who are at school.

C1

You are going to hear two students, Liam and Jade, discussing university life. Read the statements about them, then listen and tick (✔) the correct ones.

Liam   1   ... is studying science.
         2   ... works in the lab for eight hours a day.
         3   ... thinks he works harder than Jade.
Jade   4   ... is planning to miss her next lecture.
         5   ... doesn't have to go to all her lectures.
         6   ... spends every weekend studying.

C2

Listen again and choose the exact words (A, B or C) used by the speakers.

1   A   I've just got time before my next lecture.
     B   There's just time before the lecture.
     C   I'm just in time for the lesson.

2   A   There are two men with us for that.
     B   It's too much money for us.
     C   There are too many of us for that.

3   A   It's so relaxing doing arts.
     B   Things are so relaxed for you arts people.
     C   This is so relaxing for you and Art.

4   A   Things are twice as hard for you.
     B   My work's twice as hard as yours.
     C   I think I work twice as hard as you do.

5   A   What happened last week then?
     B   How about last weekend then?
     C   What about last weekend then?

D

PRONUNCIATION PRACTICE: Word stress

It is very important to stress parts of words correctly because if you don't, people may not understand you. Listen and repeat after the speaker.

1   interesting   telephone   awfully   letter   secretary   sandwich   finish   project
2   potato   tomato   ridiculous   amusing   employer   banana   graffiti   reporter
3   weekend   hotel   shampoo   engineer   mayonnaise   kangaroo   referee

Where does the stress come in each of the three groups of words?

Now listen and repeat these sentences after the speaker.

The secretary received an awfully interesting letter from her employer.
The engineer spent a quiet weekend in a hotel, before finishing his project.
Would you like mayonnaise in your tomato sandwich?

21 WHAT'S THE PROBLEM?

A

Find pairs of opposite adjectives, used for describing people.

modest	talkative	cruel	quiet	energetic
nervous	tired	proud	relaxed	kind

Which words would you like people to use when describing you? Can you use these words to describe any famous people you know?

B1

A girl and a boy, Bella and Lewis, have a problem with their relationship. You are going to hear part of a radio phone-in programme, which tries to help people with their problems. First you are going to hear Bella giving *her* side of the story. Read the questions first, then listen and answer them.

1 How long have they been going out together?
2 What type of person is Lewis?
3 What was Bella trying to tell him about?
4 Why is she worried about Lewis?
5 Can you guess why Lewis is behaving like this?

B2

Now you are going to hear Lewis's side of the story. Read the questions first, then listen and answer them.

1 What is Lewis's job?
2 How does he feel in the evenings, and why?
3 How does Bella feel in the evenings, and why?
4 Why doesn't Lewis talk much? Complete the sentences.

   a) He doesn't find it easy to _____.

   b) Bella _____ too much.
5 When does he 'switch off', and why?
6 Who doesn't like Bella much, and why?

Can you help to solve their problem? Decide what advice to give Bella or Lewis and write a letter to one of them.

C1 Luke has a Russian penfriend, Alexei. Instead of writing a letter to Alexei, Luke has recorded what he wants to say on cassette. Listen and match the names to the pictures. There is one extra picture.

Auntie Joan   Dad   Josie   Granny   Mum

What is Luke's problem? Is it a real problem?

C2 Listen again and decide whether the statements are true (T) or false (F).

1 Alexei has already written to Luke.
2 Luke's father works in a restaurant kitchen.
3 Luke's mother broke her leg playing tennis.
4 Josie and Luke have different opinions about homework.
5 Luke's Granny started knitting at the age of 80.
6 Auntie Joan lives with Luke's family.
7 Auntie Joan and Spot don't have any breakfast.
8 Luke wants his family to change.

D SPEAKING PRACTICE

Here are some ways of making suggestions.

Why don't we talk about it?   *What about spending more time together?*
Shall we ask someone's advice?   *How about telling her how you feel?*
Let's discuss it now.   *Why don't you ask what the problem is?*

And here are some possible answers.

Great idea!   Yes, why not?   OK, I'll do that.   Yes, I think we should.

Think of your own suggestions. Practise them, and the answers, with a partner.

22 MONEY MATTERS

A

What words or phrases are you likely to hear or use when talking about money?
Tick (✔) the words in the box that have something to do with money.

account	coin	income	recipe	traveller's cheques
bench	credit card	lend	savings	wallpaper
bill	currently	menu	sheep	
burger	debit card	pocket money	steel	
cash	expensive	pounds	tip	

B1

You are going to hear a man telling a story. Look at the pictures first, then listen and put them in the right order.

A   B   C   D

B2

Listen again and choose from A, B, C or D to complete the sentences correctly.

1 The man and his wife were A in Italy on business.
                                       B on holiday on the French Riviera.
                                       C on holiday in Italy.

2 They were staying A in a hotel.
                         B with friends.
                         C in rooms over a restaurant.

3 The man always pays by credit card A at lunch-time.
                                             B if a meal costs a lot.
                                             C if he's with his wife.

4 He didn't have his card because A he had lost it.
                                 B someone stole it.
                                 C it was in his other trousers.

5 He didn't tell his wife he didn't A she didn't have enough money to pay.
   have the card, because   B it would spoil her birthday.
                                   C she might be angry with him.

6 The meal plus tip cost A more than 180,000 lire.
                          B less than 180,000 lire.
                          C 180,000 lire exactly.

C1

You are going to hear a phone call to a bank. Read the questions, then listen and answer them.

1 Which bank is it?   3 What is the speaker's name?
2 What is the speaker phoning about?   4 What will the bank do now?

C2

These sentences from the phone call are in the wrong order. Listen again and put them in the correct order.

A You want some details, yes, right, I'm Victoria P. Brane, got that?
B And the card number's 4989 1662 3972 1408.
C Hello, is that the Midland Bank, the emergency help line?
D So can you cancel it or something, you know, whatever?
E At least I *think* I've lost it, but maybe it was stolen.
F So is that it – you're going to cancel my card and send me a new one?
G Victoria like the queen or the station, OK?
H Oh good – look, this really *is* an emergency.
I Anyway, I haven't got it any more.
J Then P for, well, I won't tell you what it's for, it's such a silly name, and then Brane, that's B.R.A.N.E.
K The thing is, I've lost my card, my debit card, you know.
L Then I won't have to pay if somebody else uses it, that's how it works, isn't it?

D

SPEAKING PRACTICE

Here is an 'alphabet shopping' game to help improve your vocabulary – and memory!

The first person starts by saying, '*I went into town yesterday and bought an APPLE*' (or other word beginning with A). The second person says, '*I went into town yesterday and bought an APPLE and a BOOK*' (or other word beginning with B). The next person says, '*I went into town and bought an APPLE, a BOOK and a COMPUTER.*' The game continues round the class, using all the letters from A to Z. You can play this game on your own, too.

Listening tip

Listen for the rising and falling tunes of English conversation. If the voice falls at the end of a sentence, it means the speaker has finished talking, but if the voice goes up at the end of a sentence, you know that the speaker is expecting an answer from you, or perhaps hasn't finished speaking yet.

23 FINDING YOUR WAY

A

Match the questions to the answers.

1 Could you tell me where I can find a taxi?
2 Could you tell me the way to the bus station?
3 Is it far?
4 What number bus should I take for the museum?

A Yes, turn left and it's at the bottom of the hill.
B I think it's the 27A, or the 5B.
C There are some waiting in North Street.
D No, only five minutes' walk.

B1

You are going to hear someone giving directions. Listen and number the places in the box in the order that you hear them.

bank	crossroads	roundabout
church	Dyke Road	Royal Alexandra Hospital
Clifton Road	MacBurgers	station
Clock Tower	roadworks	traffic lights

B2

Listen again and fill in Clifton Road and Dyke Road on the map, and mark the suggested route.

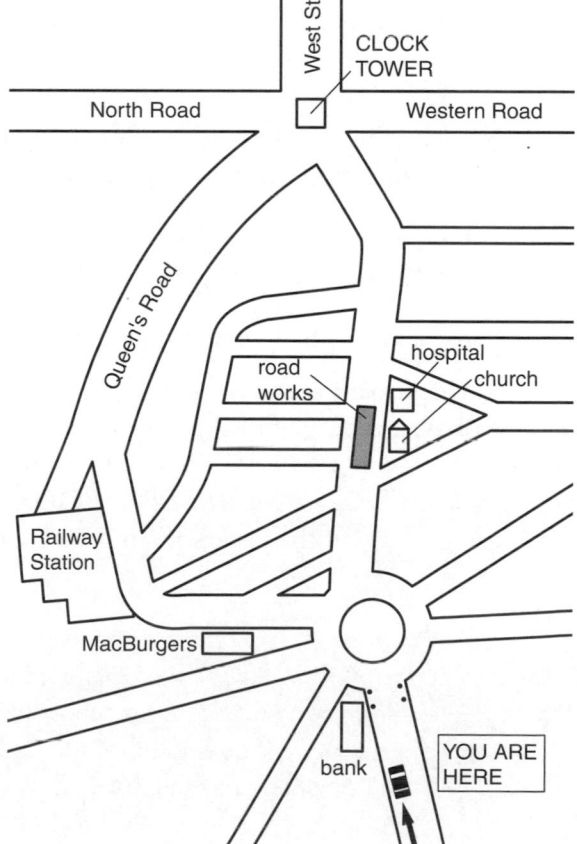

C1

You are going to hear two people talking about losing their way. Listen to the man and answer questions 1–3. Then listen to the woman and answer questions 4–6.

1 Where were the man and his friend?
2 How were they travelling?
3 How many times did they see the same policeman?
4 How was the woman travelling?
5 What was she looking for?
6 Did she take the driver's advice?

Which story does the picture show?

C2

Listen to the two people again and complete the sentences.

1 It was hard to find the hotel, because _____.

2 When the policeman saw them for the second time, _____.

3 In the end, one of the policemen _____.

4 The woman didn't know the way to the hostel, so _____.

5 The driver advised her not _____.

6 Unfortunately, she _____, so she got lost.

7 The driver and the policeman both _____.

8 The man and the woman were both helped _____.

D

SPEAKING PRACTICE

With a partner, practise asking the way and giving directions to these places.

1 the nearest post office in your town
2 the tourist office
3 the main railway station
4 the hospital
5 the nearest bank/bookshop/newsagent's

Listening tip

Remember that many English words have the same sound, but a different spelling and a different meaning, for example:

tail, tale   see, sea   flower, flour   heard, herd   road, rode   break, brake
been, bean   made, maid   father, farther   leak, leek   piece, peace

Just concentrate on what the words mean in the sentence that you are listening to.

24 PEOPLE

A   Find pairs of opposite adjectives, used for describing people.

shy	sad	kind	mean	cruel	quiet
polite	happy	unsure	noisy	unselfish	
rude	sociable	generous	confident	selfish	

What kind of person are you? Describe yourself, using some of the adjectives in the box.

B1   You are going to hear descriptions of five people. Look at the pictures, then listen and number the objects in the order that you hear them.

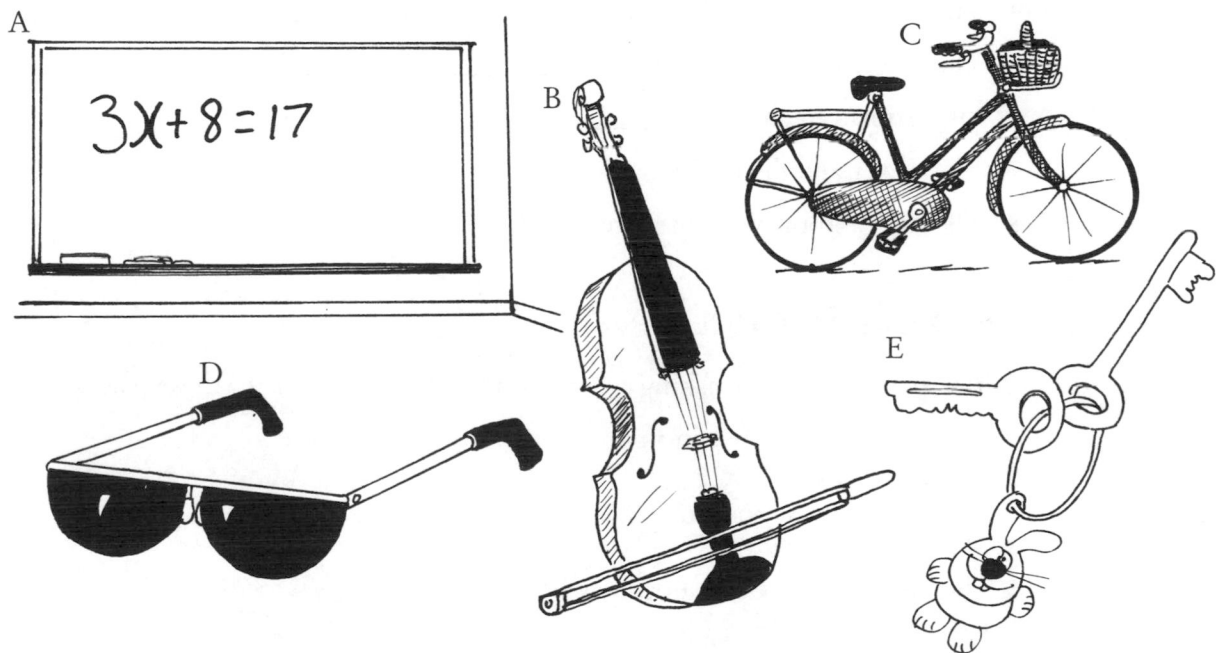

A $$3X + 8 = 17$$

B2   Read the statements, then listen again and choose the correct statement for each person. There are two extra statements.

1	Claudia	A	... earns a good salary as a musician.
2	Jim	B	... often goes shopping.
3	Miss Henderson	C	... wants to look fashionable.
4	Gary	D	... likes animals.
5	Mr Lewis	E	... believes in luck.
		F	... doesn't worry about money.
		G	... was good at the job.

C1 You are going to hear some more information about the five people. Listen and complete the paragraphs, using ONE word for each gap.

1 Claudia comes from Dunbar, (1) _____ Edinburgh. She is (2) _____ years old. She comes from a (3) _____ family. She finds it very (4) _____ to meet people, and doesn't like (5) _____ out.

2 Jim's parents are both (1)_____. The whole family are very (2) _____, and they play in (3) _____ together. He always says (4) _____ to you when he sees you, and even holds (5) _____ open.

3 Miss Henderson had a (1) _____ once, a long time (2) _____. But she never got (3) _____ because she had to look after her elderly (4) _____. So she gave up her freedom and her (5) _____ of getting married.

4 Gary spends a lot of money on (1) _____. Luckily, he has a good (2) _____, with a high salary – he works in his father's company. He spends money on his friends, too, especially on their (3) _____.

5 Everyone at the local school (1) _____ Mr Lewis. He was a (2) _____ teacher. Now he's retired, he doesn't seem to have any (3) _____, and he spends a lot of time on his (4) _____. I don't think he looks very (5) _____.

C2 Listen again and choose the adjective from Exercise A which best describes each person.

1 Claudia _____   4 Gary _____

2 Jim _____   5 Mr Lewis _____

3 Miss Henderson _____

D SPEAKING PRACTICE

Find out about people you are interested in. Ask these questions.

What's his/her name?   *How old is he/she?*
Where does he/she live?   *What does he/she do?*
What is he/she interested in? *What kind of person is he/she?*

Ask a partner about   (a) his/her brother or sister   (b) his/her parents   (c) his/her best friend (d) his/her teacher.

Listening tip   Talking to English-speaking people is a good way of practising your listening. Even if they talk fast, try to understand, and ask questions if necessary. Taking part in real conversations will make you more confident when listening.

25 HAPPY FAMILIES

A **Think about or discuss these questions about your family.**

What is your family like? How many brothers and sisters have you got? Are they older or younger than you? Do your grandparents, or your aunts, uncles and cousins live with you?

B1 **Look at the pictures, then listen to four people talking about their families. Match the speakers 1–4 to the pictures.**

B2 **Listen again and decide which sentence (A, B or C) best describes the way the people feel about their families.**

Speaker 1	A	He liked living in a quiet house.
	B	He didn't enjoy being an only child.
	C	He remembers his parents laughing a lot.
Speaker 2	A	She likes living with her cousins.
	B	She wishes her sisters could live with them.
	C	She thinks their house is too big.
Speaker 3	A	Living away from home makes him unhappy.
	B	It's not easy living with an old lady.
	C	He enjoys his grandmother's cooking.
Speaker 4	A	She wants to help her mother.
	B	She often tells her brothers what to do.
	C	Things have changed now that there's a new dog in the house.

How do you get on with your family? Do you ever argue with your brothers and sisters or your parents? If so, what do you argue about? And who usually wins the argument?

C1   You are going to hear a woman talking about her family. Look at the family tree, then listen and fill in the gaps with the names in the box.

Arthur	Diana	Dorothy	Helen	Jeff	Joseph
Kathleen	Keith	Maria	Sarah	Susan	Tina

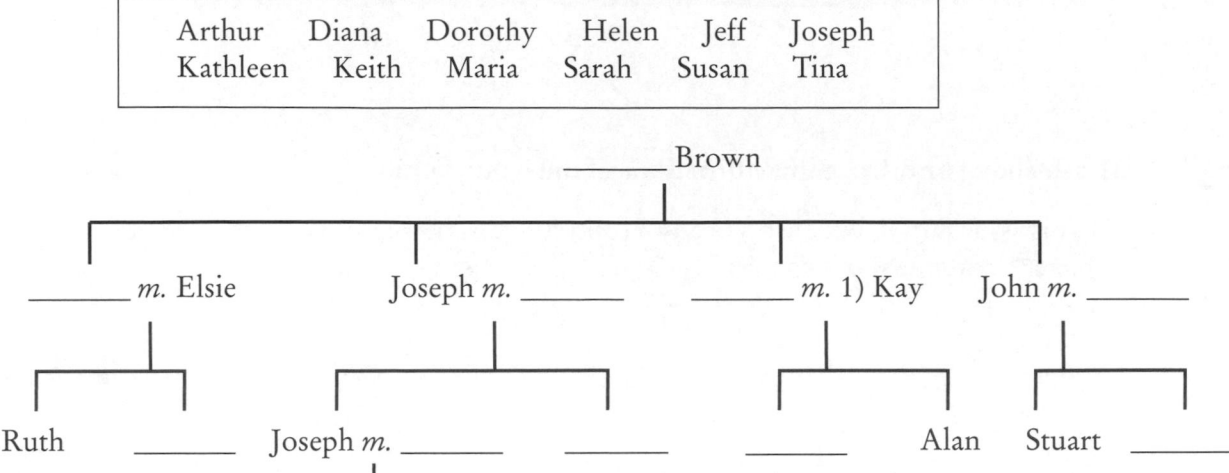

_____ Brown

_____ *m.* Elsie   Joseph *m.* _____   _____ *m.* 1) Kay   John *m.* _____

Ruth   _____   Joseph *m.* _____   _____   _____   Alan   Stuart   _____

m. 2) _____

_____   Alison   (*m.* = married)

C2   Listen again and answer the questions.

1   What relation is Helen to Keith?
2   What relation is Jeff to the speaker?
3   What is the speaker's name?
4   What relation are Sarah and Alison to the speaker?
5   How many people in the family share the same name, and what is it?

D   **PRONUNCIATION PRACTICE:**   Verb endings

Listen to the ten sentences and choose the verb you hear from the pair in each box. Watch out for the different endings of English verb forms.

1 play / played	2 watch / watches	3 run / runs	4 cook / cooked

5 take / takes	6 pass / passed	7 wash / washed

8 write / writes	9 walks / walked	10 looks / looked

Listen again and repeat the sentences after the speaker, making sure you pronounce the verb endings correctly.

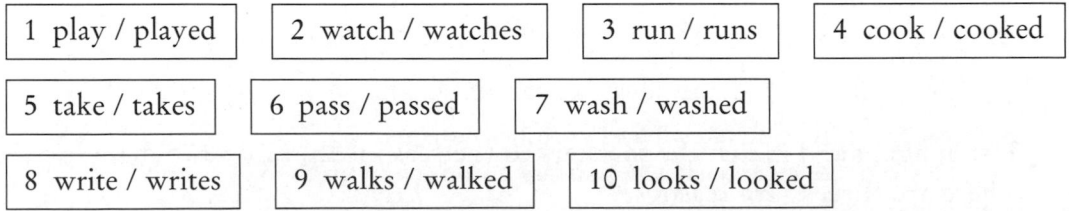

Listening tip

When you are listening to English, keep eye contact with the speaker. Use your face to show you are interested. You can also help the speaker along by nodding your head from time to time, or by saying encouraging things like 'Really?', 'Well!', 'Did you?'

26 THE WORLD OF WORK

A Match the pictures to eight of the jobs in the box.

baker	gardener	teacher
doctor	greengrocer	vet
farmer	lifeguard	waitress
firefighter	secretary	window-cleaner

Would you like to do any of these jobs? What jobs do people in your family do?
Choose two of the jobs and compare them. What are their advantages and disadvantages?

B1 You are going to hear four speakers talking about their work. Look at the jobs in the box above, then listen and tick (✔) the ones that you hear.

B2 Listen again and match the speakers to the reasons they give for changing their jobs. There are three extra reasons.

Speaker 1   A ... wanted more free time.
Speaker 2   B ... did not like the boss.
Speaker 3   C ... wanted to earn more money.
Speaker 4   D ... moved to another town.
                E ... wanted to work with animals.
                F ... got married.
                G ... had an accident.

What do you think are the best reasons for changing jobs?

C1

You are going to hear a man talking about his life and career. Read the questions, then listen and answer them.

1 Which languages can he speak?
2 What nationality was his mother?
3 Did he enjoy teaching?
4 Why did he become a writer?

C2

These sentences describe his life so far, but they are in the wrong order. Listen again and put them in the right order.

A He moved to Paris.
B He taught foreign languages to private pupils.
C He bought a large house overlooking the sea.
D He won a prize for his writing.
E He was born in a city in the United Kingdom.
F His best pupil was a count.
G He studied at Munich University.
H He became a writer of detective stories.
I He moved to Austria.

D

PRONUNCIATION PRACTICE: Similar sounds

Listen to some phrases from the recording and choose the correct word or phrase you hear from each pair in the box.

1	grown up / growing up	7	German / Germany
2	Chichester / Manchester	8	in a palace / Indianapolis
3	Harris / Paris	9	writer / lighter
4	France / French	10	1919 / 1990
5	Austria / Australia	11	Turkey / Torquay
6	teacher / preacher	12	walked home / worked at home

Listen and repeat these words or phrases after the speaker, making sure your pronunciation is very clear.

Listening tip

Don't just listen to the words, listen for clues in the tone of voice. Is the speaker angry, or bored, or sad? Look at people's body language, which could help you to understand what they really mean. For example, someone receiving flowers might say, *'Oh, you shouldn't have!'* If you just listen to the words, you might think that giving the flowers was wrong or a mistake, but if you look at their body language, you will realise how pleased they are.

27 WHAT LOVELY WEATHER!

A

Match the symbols to the kind of weather that they represent. You are going to use them in Exercise B1.

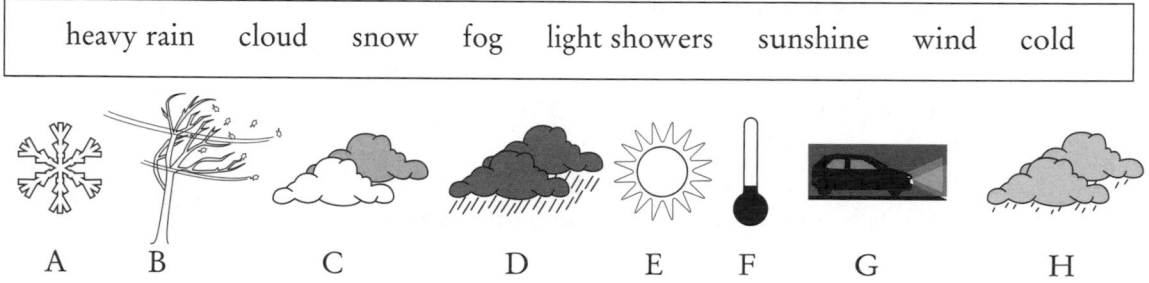

| heavy rain | cloud | snow | fog | light showers | sunshine | wind | cold |

A   B   C   D   E   F   G   H

B1

Look at the map of Scotland, then listen to the weather forecast. Write one of the letters (A–H) from above beside each place on the map, to show what kind of weather it is going to get.

B2

Listen again and answer the questions.

1 Which place will have the most sunshine tomorrow?
2 What will the top temperature be there?
3 Why must you be careful if you're driving in Edinburgh?
4 Is it unusual for the outer Hebrides to be rainy?
5 What will the maximum temperature be in Glasgow tomorrow?
6 What kind of weather will the Orkney Islands get soon (not tomorrow)?
7 What kind of weather can the Scots expect for next week?

C1 You are going to hear two neighbours talking about a recent holiday. Read the questions, then listen and answer them.

1 Where did Grace go on holiday?
2 What was the weather problem she experienced?
3 Did she stay in the same hotel for the whole holiday?
4 Which weather conditions does she complain of?
5 What was the weather like at home while she was away?

C2 Listen to these phrases from the recording and choose the correct phrase you hear from each pair in the box.

1	for the four weeks / for the first week	7	poor you / for you
2	hear about it / hereabouts	8	we want it to / we wanted to do
3	awful tornado / or full tornado	9	it's a real leaf / it's a relief
4	to another hotel / to the other hotel	10	I can tell you / I can't tell you
5	nobody was heard / nobody was hurt	11	on the home / on the whole
6	really quite cold / really quiet cold	12	just very cold / usefully cold

D SPEAKING PRACTICE

This is the sort of thing people often say when talking about the weather.

A: What a lovely day!
A: It rained terribly hard yesterday, didn't it?
A: It's never been as cold as this in June before!

B: Yes, it is, isn't it?
B: Yes, it did, didn't it?
B: No, it hasn't, has it?

The politeness rule is that, in a conversation about the weather, you almost always agree with the other person.

What should you say if someone talks to you about the weather? Match the sentences to the replies and then practise short conversations about the weather with a partner.

1 *We had a much better summer in 1976!*
2 *It did snow heavily yesterday.*
3 *I think it's going to rain.*
4 *It was cloudier this morning.*
5 *It's never rained so much in April before!*

A *Yes, it did, didn't it?*
B *No, it hasn't, has it?*
C *Yes, we did, didn't we?*
D *Yes, it is, isn't it?*
E *Yes, it was, wasn't it?*

Listening tip

Just before a listening test, make sure you talk to your friends in English, or if you can't do that, think in English. Ask and answer questions in your head, for example:

How long is this test going to last?
How many people are there in the room?
What kind of vocabulary will there be in the test?

This will make it easier for you to 'tune in' to listening in English.

28 GAME, SET AND MATCH!

A Match the pictures to eight of these sporting activities.

basketball	rugby	baseball	riding	darts
hockey	tennis	skiing	golf	snooker

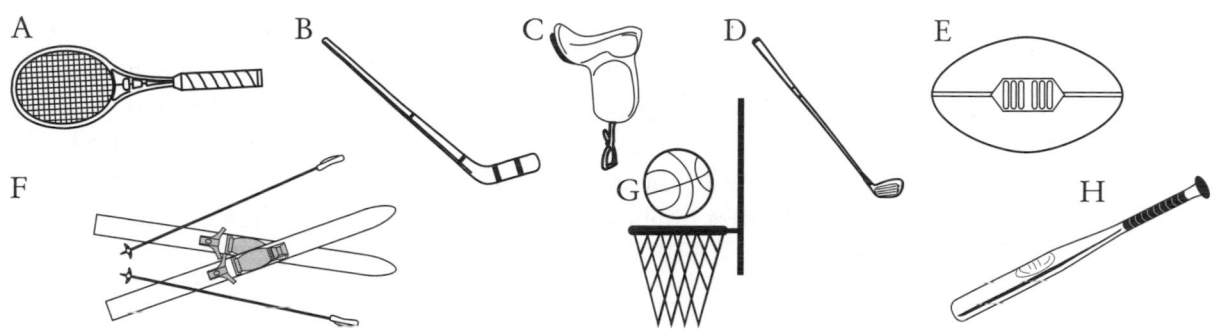

What is your favourite sport? Which is the most popular sport in your country?
Do you prefer watching or playing?

B1 You are going to hear four sports people talking about their lives. Listen and tick (✔)
the words that you hear.

champion	football	manager	practice	team
cup	income	match	prize	training
exercise	lifestyle	money	sport	trips

B2 Listen again and fill in the table.

Name	Sport	What he/she is doing now	Future plans/sports events
1 Brian			
2 Hazel			
3 Dylan			
4 Matt			

C1

You are going to hear a radio reporter giving the commentary for a match. Look at the words in the box. Which sport are they all connected with? What do they mean?

umpire	love	game	set	match	serve

Read the questions, then listen and answer them.

1 What nationality are the players?
2 Who does the reporter expect to win?
3 Why is this an important game?
4 What happens at the end of the game?

C2

Listen again and choose from A, B, C or D to complete the sentences correctly.

1 Rosie Finch is _____ than Lulu Bassett.
  A older   B richer   C fitter   D taller

2 _____ are watching.
  A Rosie's mother and father   C Lulu's manager and husband
  B Rosie's sister and boyfriend   D Lulu's best friend and manager

3 Rosie wins the game because of _____
  A her fast serve.   C her new racquet.
  B her manager's advice.   D her fans.

4 There's a fight because _____
  A the umpire makes a mistake.   C it's a very hot day.
  B Rosie's boyfriend doesn't   D Lulu thinks the umpire is wrong.
    like Lulu's husband.

D

PRONUNCIATION PRACTICE: Singular and plural nouns

You can add an -s to most nouns in English, to make them plural, but there are many where you can't do this, for example, *child, children*. Listen and repeat the singular and plural nouns.

Now listen to some individual words and write S for singular or P for plural.

1 ____	4 ____	7 ____	10 ____	13 ____	16 ____
2 ____	5 ____	8 ____	11 ____	14 ____	17 ____
3 ____	6 ____	9 ____	12 ____	15 ____	18 ____

Final listening tips

1 Try to predict what words you might hear. Think about the topic.
2 Look at the speaker, his or her lips, and his or her body language.
3 Concentrate hard on the speaker's words.
4 If it's a recording, listen again as often as you need to.
5 If it's a live conversation, don't be afraid to ask for help, or ask the speaker to repeat.

PRONUNCIATION BANK

A Many words sound similar in English. Look at these explanations and see if you can work out what the similar-sounding words are. Then listen and choose the correct explanation of the word you hear.

1 A like *his*, but for a girl
   B opposite of *there*
   C what grows on your head

2 A plural of *was*
   B fighting between countries
   C put on (clothes)

3 A a special shoe for cold or wet weather
   B a small ship, for sailing or rowing
   C paid for

4 A a cook
   B most important
   C opposite of *expensive*

5 A to go away
   B opposite of *death*
   C opposite of *die*

6 A unhappy
   B spoken
   C last letter of the alphabet

7 A a new thought
   B something perfect
   C identity card

8 A longer than a postcard
   B recently
   C opposite of *earlier*

B You may think you recognise a short word as part of a longer word, but the pronunciation and stress are often different. Look at these pairs of words, then listen and repeat them after the speaker.

please, pleasure   she, shell
cup, cupboard   fat, fatal
pot, potato   car, caravan
hop, hoping   plan, plant

C Many words in English have silent letters. Listen and circle the silent letters in these words. (Some of the words have more than one silent letter.)

walk   castle
bird   cupboard
thumb   hour
calm   write
why   leopard

Now listen and repeat the words after the speaker.

D See what a difference one letter can make to the pronunciation of a word! Listen and repeat these words after the speaker.

red, redo	rat, rate	own, gown
sit, site	bath, bathe	mat, mast
mad, made	hall, hallo	cost, coast
lose, loose	face, farce	hot, host

E Place names often sound quite different from the way they are written. Listen and repeat these place names after the speaker.

Delhi	Durham	Blenheim	Birmingham
Minneapolis	Seattle	Montreal	Reading
Edinburgh	Peterborough	Pittsburgh	Johannesburg
Leicester	Worcester	Gloucester	Bicester
Bournemouth	Houston	Vancouver	Melbourne
Salisbury	Canterbury	Newbury	Shrewsbury
Brighton	Kingston	Wellington	Washington
Norwich	Greenwich	Harwich	Warwick
Yorkshire	Cheshire	Hampshire	Shropshire

F Here are some more place names from around the world. Listen to the way they are usually pronounced in British English, and repeat them after the speaker.

Argentina	Japan	Egypt	Uruguay
Australia	Europe	the E.U.	the U.S.A.
Dublin	Paris	Florence	Geneva
Moscow	Munich	Berlin	Madrid
Cambridge	Manchester	Glasgow	London
Heathrow Airport	Oxford Circus	the River Thames	Trafalgar Square

G Look at these words which English has 'borrowed' from other languages. Then listen and repeat them after the speaker.

tycoon	marmalade	yogurt	pyjamas
yacht	garage	hotel	karaoke
sauna	mosquito	carafe	kiosk
chauffeur	duvet	siesta	anorak
macho	tattoo	skiing	bistro

INDEX

PRONUNCIATION

SPEAKING